salmonpoetry

Publishing Irish & International

Poetry Since 1981

Salmon Poetry gratefully acknowledges the support of
The Arts Council / An Chomhairle Ealaíon
towards the publication of this book

RANDOMER

Colm Keegan

Published in 2018 by
Salmon Poetry
Cliffs of Moher, County Clare, Ireland
Website: www.salmonpoetry.com
Email: info@salmonpoetry.com

ISBN 978-1-912561-02-5

COVER DESIGN: *Ray Glasheen – www.rayglasheen.com*
TYPESETTING: *Siobhán Hutson*

Printed in Ireland by Sprint Print

Salmon Poetry gratefully acknowledges the support of
The Arts Council / An Chomhairle Ealaíon

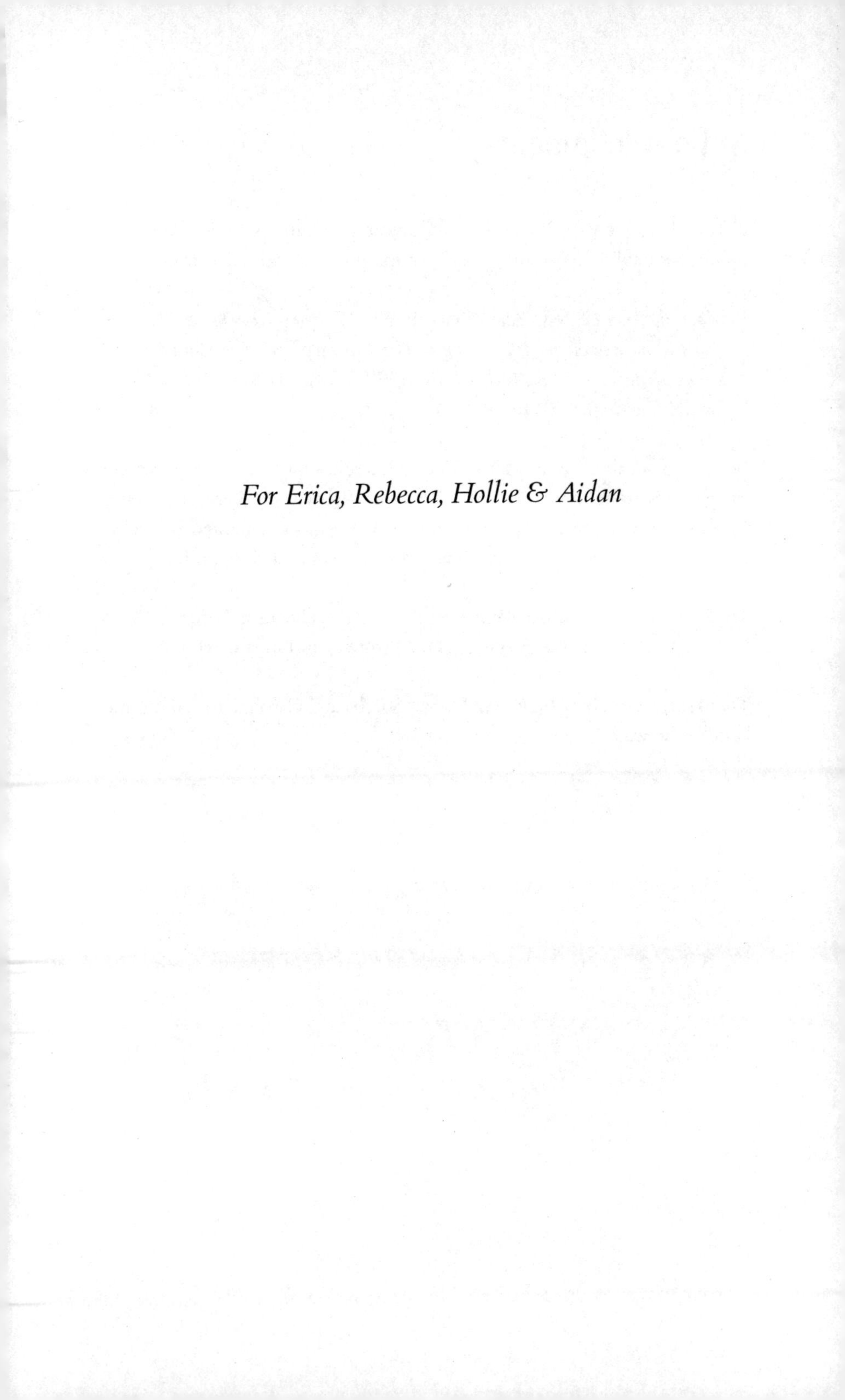

For Erica, Rebecca, Hollie & Aidan

Acknowledgments

Acknowledgements are due to the following publications, radio shows and events, for publishing or airing some of the poems in this collection:

Reading the Future (ed. Alan Hayes), *The Galway Review*, *Selfies and Portraits – an anthology*, *Bare Hands*, *The Stinging Fly*, *The Brown Bread Mixtape*, *Nighthawks at the Cobalt*, *Arena* (RTE Radio 1), *Culture File* (RTE Radio 1), *The Business* (RTE Radio 1).

My thanks are also due to DLR LexIcon for a residency in 2014, from where I began this collection; to Pauline Duffy and Rebecca Ford at Collinstown Community College for the very special base I have there; and to Helen McMahon and all at Clondalkin library for their continued support.

Special thanks to Stephen Kennedy, Aiden O'Reilly, Erin Fornoff, Brian Kirk, Kalle Ryan, Elaine Feeney, John Murphy, and Linda Devlin.

Thanks to my mother Maureen, Donal, Sorcha and Caroline for taking me back to the well.

Contents

1

Murder Road

Turn up at 11pm and suggest an impromptu workshop,
nothing too heavy, an icebreaker, something about
sharing secrets, fictions, Russian roulette with words
where nobody knows where the truth bullet is, and it works,
but it works too well and you're like fucking hell
this is an overwhelming level of admission, dark truths
and vulnerability in the room like a coiling mess of broken
electrical wires, sparks everywhere – out of our mouths
and out of our eyes, because this is more than ice that's breaking.

The veil between what we present to the world and what we
really are has faded away and what do we do
with all this? And I come up with a desperate solution,
holding the heavy secrets in my hand I say I'm going
to set them on fire, I'll burn them all, and I leave.

I go out into the starlight and walk up the boreen
to a stone bridge, dark trees moving in the wind,
and standing alone on a Killarney road I light my little fire,
and smoke rises and a crow jumps in the branches and screams,
and the darkness is alive because this one woke crow is letting
his whole murder know that the fire is coming, and the trees
are wild with the nighttime chorus. The secret fire,
the silver grey tendrils of burnt poems and admissions,
a terror to all these cawing birds. Such a glorious disturbance.

And if anyone walked by right then I'd be like, "Yeah, how's it goin'
I'm a special arsonist. My job is waking the crows.
I take people's problems and set them free, dark spells on the breeze.
No big deal, I think I do it better than most.
What's the craic with you anyway man, any smokes?"

January Train

Fields of trees encased in frozen dew.
The sun a sullen distant heatless disc.
Tractors in a line retired between
cold foreground and an almost lost horizon.

A smattering of slick and sharded ponds.
Sheep, a flock of huffing moving heat.
Buckled fence all bent like broken teeth.
A swollen river eating up a field.

Through the Norman shock of Ballinasloe
the train rolls over sleepers eight years old.
Ivy covered chimney plays mute host
to a starving winter crow.

Beauty in a row of frozen trees.
Copse of colour muted by new fog.
Each drop a fractal gem escaping frost.

Uiscebot's Biography

Uiscebot writes what's on his mind
and lies when he says
that everything's a lie.

Uiscebot's grandparents spoke
like they were choking on boxty,
were born on a potato that exploded
in the big bang of paddywhackery
that propelled them to invent Christianity
in Slovenia, drill for Guinness in Africa
before harvesting the teeth of the dead
on the silent mist covered battlefields
of the Napoleonic wars
as fuel for American (manifest) dentistry.

Obviously, Uiscebot's a conspiracy theorist
who believes in Jesus, and all his
cultural carbon copies including
Tom Joad, Neo from the Matrix and Spongebob.

Uiscebot's like Dostoevsky online,
stops at traffic lights in Grand Theft Auto,
thinks nothing of garroting the traffic warden
for the experience and the level up points.

Uiscebot is dropping loads of list poems.
Eats clichés for breakfast, capiche?
Massages your cinema gland
with explosions and hollywood malapropisms.
Is a 'Tired of getting sand kicked in your face?'
comic book ad coming at you
in the shape of a ninja star.

Uiscebot's favourite word is And.

AND!

Despite his face
Uiscebot's nose
has been shaved off
by the IMF grindstone
and like a pliant little ploughman dope
he's returned to the yoke.

Uiscebot has swallowed every celebrity
sex video in the known universe.

Uiscebot is the culmination
of three million years of internet dating,
dreams of female marines having orgasms
on his computer screen and calling his name.

Uiscebot has crossed the line,
cries when his avatars die.
Safe search is off for poor Uiscebot.

Uiscebot is a a girl and a boy and the
rainbow of grey in between
and a hermaphrodite in the
middle with a guillotine.

Uiscebot has a thing for the dark side of the museum.

Uiscebot is forever zooming in on the Mandelbrot set.
He thinks fractals are haunted by the Devil.
Can't see any difference between
the search box and the confession box.
Watch what you say, the Priests are still listening

Uiscebot ignores the weatherman.
He knows it's not raining anymore.
Those are icebergs falling from the sky.

Uiscebot's coming soon
all over your TV.
Has two TVs for feet actually.
Is on his knees
crawling along your eyeball
stalks to live in your brain.

Uiscebot believes that
we are skimmer stones
tossed across the sea of time.
That we are a quantum sort of humanity –
that every room is both full
and informed by its own emptiness,
our applause and our laughter
both here and long gone
and going on in our descendants' heads.

Swallowers

Why do we do it?
Push it in so far.
All those hours of practice
for cuts and scabs.

All that forced opening
for some cheap applause
and a standing ovation
for blood on the sword.

Newborn

The hardness of the air compared
to where I've been is
a million tiny needles
pushing into my skin.

In a too big room
and the boom boom boom boom
of a bouncing ball
or is it pain
or is it a drum?

And there's the prototype.
The progenitor.
The mighty one.
The metaphor.
The father.

And what does he say?
He says shut up fucking crying.

The laughing gangster.
The soldier.
The bastard maker.

I am too young to speak
But for some reason I understand.

I have just left my mother.
This room is cold.
The air kills my skin.

This is Ballymun.
This life I'm in.

1975.
The worst year of the troubles.
274 people died.
I'm crying for my life.

At my christening
I will be named
after a man whose head was blown off.

I am screaming
screaming
screaming
for the womb.

Punk Mother

1

The alarm on the phone goes off.
Its tone reminds me of your sing song
voice calling me to wake when I was four.

A memory from the time before
I could name time, name
things, or name myself
back when there was just you and me.

Nobody has ever made me feel
as special as when I heard you call my name.

It hurts to admit that time moves on.
We're not those younger people anymore.
Things have a way of changing.

If I could say what it was that caused it all
I couldn't just name one thing.

There's a pain in my heart when I think on it.
All that's been lost in the spin of this world.
How old you look, how worn out by it all.

In a corner of myself that I learned to neglect
you're there.

2

A cool punk mother
in our Ballymun flat, that summer.

Outside the wire-frame glass;
a shadow made of leather and testosterone
banging on the door for what you owe.

Inside, your green army style turtleneck jumper
that I dreamt you died in once, you shiver,
deliver heat to me through your cool clothes.

There was a safety pin in your red tartan dress.
And I want to forget everything else
but our closeness as we hid near the press.

Usurper

I saw you coming that night.
It was a long time coming this fight.
You thought you had power on your side,
but my hands had the momentum of pain.

The hole you bore into my chest
by poking and poking with your finger
fed a dynamo that spun so relentless,
with the speed of a hummingbird's wings.

It felt good to stick my thumbs in your mouth.
It felt good to cut my knuckles on your teeth.
It felt good to let the blackness out,
you'd spent years pouring into me.

Now I no longer hear crying in the wind.
I no longer dread the screams of my mother.
I no longer feel trapped in my bedroom.
I made bastards of my sister and brother.

Lie Bird

My mother never saw the bird.
My mother never saw the garden.
My mother never saw my father
do something so kind.
After my father's hands around
my mother's throat that's all she saw.

The bird is frightened
we trapped it using bread and
the red lid from a linen basket and
some rope tied to a stick we tugged
when the bird was dumb or
hungry enough to get caught.

I have my hands around the bird
I have my hands around the bird and
it is silent and it is light and
I know what's in its eyes and
I know my father says to me
its bones are hollow. It's made of air.
And I know it is a sparrow.

But now my father's gone and
the man who took his place says
there was no sparrow, he says
it was a starling.
The black thing pecked the hands off me.

This Voice

This voice was born in 1975, in Holles Street hospital, where it cried out with scores of others, joined in with a symphony of tiny voices demanding nourishment, touch, warmth.

This voice belonged to a toddler in Ballymun, then a four year old, screaming cause it was locked in a lift, or howling at the seagulls, spiralling down the concrete steps out into the roads up into the air to mix with the jets flying overhead.

This voice left north Dublin, became part of the southside that doesn't get to be called the southside.

Jobstown Tallaght, Foxdene Clondalkin, Leighlin Road Crumlin.

This voice became something to be judged, the sound of the scanger, the scumbag.

This voice once tried but couldn't rise above those titles, internalised the tribal jibes that might bounce off a thicker skin.

This voice's balls dropped as it took all that on board, this voice was often part of the mob, screaming abuse at authority, teachers, coppers.

This voice started to talk about love, this voice tried to talk women's knickers off, but this voice in the presence of women, was usually lost.

Then this voice grew up, grew older, some babies were born – this voice sang lullabies, became stronger, learned how to give orders, instructions, took on the soft tone of forgiveness when needed. This voice matured. It carried more.

This voice found a place to work, roared above the machines on the factory floor, sold lies down a mobile phone for profit. Talked about believing in things that it didn't believe like low hanging fruit and going fucking forward. This voice couldn't survive there for long. This voice didn't have the right pitch for that nonsense.

This voice talked teens into kayaking, directed them in small plastic boats, showed them the Dublin's mother, the Liffey, thought them its song:

You can't control the flow,
you must follow where it goes.
Don't try to block it for too long,
without release, it overflows.

This voice owes so much to books, how they transmit ideas – words that hit like a punch, like a bullet shot from a gun, or like a kiss, like falling snow dropped onto water.

This voice surrendered to words, bent down at the altar of them.

Where this different voice bubbled up, like a river after enough rain.

And then this voice found the stage, joined the rumble of an underground something exploding across Dublin, something that saw no lines between performer and audience, something anarchic, a bit punk.

This voice could be absorbed by the establishment, like all voices are absorbed, but once it knows its place isn't inside the castle, it'll keep on.

This voice has travelled, a vast distance, not just across time, but across space, where it was sent from a microphone, transformed into a billion digital bits, pinged up to a satellite dish, back down and straight into your kitchen where it moves through you as sound waves, resonates in the echo chamber of your ribcage, and transforms into synaptic flashes that electrify your neural pathways.

This voice could sit there for years, or for just a few minutes.

This voice is not the word of the lord, this voice is not the received pronunciation, just the word of mouth.

This voice hopes to make a difference.

This voice knows it could be
choked out, strangled, gagged,
burned at the stake,
beaten, shot, stabbed
for saying what it wants to say
but stamp it out, quell it, kill it and
it will just erupt in a different place.

Because this voice isn't mine.
This voice is the cliche of the green
shoot that cracks open the pavement.
This voice is not just me, it's you.
And it's screaming at you to tell the truth.
And it's not going to leave you alone,
even when you keep your trap shut,
it goes around and around in your head.
This voice knows what you want to say.
It won't stop until it's said.

2

Springshine

The house compacted
then opening up so fast
like a popcorn kernel
or a stop motion flower
exploding with my laughter after
my four year old son's first joke –
wit like a whip crack
snapping out from his mouth.

In the hall my daughter spins
into her dream of being
a gymnast, she flips back
bends and unfurls herself.
The room is stirred with her energy,
her aura moving through the air
like slow motion orbs of water.

Her older sister has curled up
on the couch, stares into her phone,
opens herself in pixels.
Shows her feelings as letters
sent to an invisible boy.
When the tick turns green on her screen
what comes in reply is like a bomb
going off in her endocrine system.
She walks to the kitchen.

Her mother is making spaghetti Bolognese,
no frills just the sauce from a jar,
some mince.
We like it simple.
The steam of it on the walls.
The drone of the extractor fan.
The small ceremony
of cutlery thrown across the table.
The daughter helps and can't help smiling.
Her mother doesn't know why
but smiles as well.
This is the soft machine of our life.

Last night the house was warm without the heating on.
This morning sunlight woke us one by one
and the noise of a teen hurtling across
the green outside, gunning a scrambler,
accelerating, feeling the wind in his hair.

Inside the engine, small bursts of fire
while his tyres run over the grass.
In the dark beneath this all
new bulbs push hard against the clay.

Decking

You bought it with borrowed money,
hired some foreign bodies to install it
while building onto the house you spent
so much time telling your friends about
(how much it cost, how they ought not
fall anywhere short of how far you've gone
doing unto others what others do unto you.)

Off you vaulted yourself, into the realm
of credit, the second mortgage, the life
forever inventing itself on the billboard.
You'd only finished constructing it all and
then, like this shock of freakish weather,
the ocean conveyor slowing, the ice caps melting,
the Aurora Borealis slipping down from the north;
the merry go round of easy money stopped.

All through that one lost summer like a curse,

the rain kept falling and falling

(so many cataclysmic drops per day).

And now the extension roof is leaking,

cracks creep through the walls,

and your decking won't support a single step,

is covered in reptile green slime, lies

silent like a criminal outside, waiting

to crack your coccyx, break your aging hip

or put a chip in that corruptible Irish

smile of yours that started it all.

Zugunruhe

this is the bird with plumage

evolved to wink in the sun

this is the Emlen Funnel

an upside down cone

where the bird is imprisoned

this is the planetarium sky

refracted in the birds frantic eye

as it tries to migrate

its wings soaked in ink

for it to draw its own trail

which is noted down

the process repeated

the sky

rotated

Emlen Funnel: Cone shaped cage used to study bird movement.
Zugunruhe: The migratory drive in animals, especially birds.

Austerity

Searching for a symbol this is all we've got:
two slaughtered animals, hooves chopped off,
heads removed, insides gone,
hanging from the back door of a rigid truck.

Searching for a symbol this is all we've got:
a black patch of grass where a family car was.
Fire engine, ambulance, tow-truck gone.
Remnants of a wheel with the rubber burned off.

This is the day when the landlord calls –
takes everything we have just to answer the phone,
takes everything we have just to pay what's owed,
takes everything we have just to make it home.

There are no signs. This is the road.
All the slaughtered animals, their insides gone.
A man slaps the shanks, tells a butcher's joke.

Con Cave

'You've gotta punch the clock,
why don't you punch your boss?' Jello Biafra

It's like a submarine
this submerged feeling,
weight pressing down.

Footsteps on the metal stairs
strengthen the sensation.

The whir of the compressor.
The stirring of commerce.

We sit here all day
turning money into pixels
and pixels into money.

We sweat into letters
made of LCD light.
The light becomes a guide
for burning lines into plates.

What is scorched in stays.
What isn't gets washed away
and a printing plate is made.

Plates print on packaging.
Packaging becomes waste.
The money is pixels again.

No windows, just aircon.
At night we never dream.

As cows are bound
to milking machines
our eyes are tied to screens.

This is the price of our security.

Scroll click.
Scroll click.
Just as it was done before.
Pushing shapes around.
Control C.
Control V.

The manager walks in
with his promoted walk.

His pen clicks loud, like a cox's roar.
Each click a silver ball
hitting another on a desk.

A bead sliding across an abacus.
A nail hammered into my brain.

So many afraid to walk out the door
because to leave means to drown in debt.

This is the cave I left.

Console

I can't remember what I lost.
Just where I was
when I stored that haul.

So heavy. It was.

(What does that mean?)

It was as if I could not walk.
I stood in an abandoned cabin.
In a snow-filled valley.
Outside a river ran beyond.

(Beyond what?)

I could hear animals,
their cries colliding
in the moonlit fog.

(Moonlit by what?)

I hid my weapons.
All my items I put down
into the blackness of a box

and out I walked.

I could not lock the door.
I never marked the spot.
I could not feel the cold.

And now the game's corrupt.
All that I saved is gone.

Anniversary

1

Familiarity breathes, unkempt

I scratch myself, belch and fart

in your presence.

The essence of our closeness is silence.

Something's up but

my eyes are in a book, a pause

but then the phone goes.

My mouth is off again running away to talk

to somebody else, ears always open

unless it's you, I watch your lips moving

put up my finger, one minute,

feign interest, a yes to the question

I didn't hear, playing catch-up

wondering what has you so animated.

What's wrong? Again? Of course

I'm listening. I'm your husband, amn't I?

You turn away, dismayed, I return to my cave

my guilt kept at bay by a promise to myself.

I'll make it up to you.

2

Dark morning, the road washed in blue.

The screaming rush through red lights.

Now alone again in the house you left

I open the fridge to the night.

Upstairs all the children are sleeping.

Bubbles gone from the water by now.

Your cigarette burned out by the sink.

Candles flickering in your absence.

A blush of heated pink.

I stand by the bath hugging my last flat can

on our first anniversary.

I can hear autumn brushing against my door

in the way the blackbirds outside sing.

Can't open the cards on our mantlepiece.

I just want to hear the jangle from your bunch of keys.

Bering Strait

i.m. Rachel Peavoy

We've been crossing this frozen ocean
snowblind in a perpetual storm.
Our tribe has endured this trial so long
we almost forget where we're from.

Beyond the horizon, our destination
hope, an approaching thaw
and here the question that burns in our gut
what to do about all that we've lost.

Sacrifices we were forced to make,
those we left so the rest could keep going.
We are bound to all that we have given up.
It lingers in our wake like a ghost.

How many fallen have we left behind,
their voices calling out in the snow?
Are we going to go back and save who we can
or keep marching for fear of the cold?

The Weight of Homelessness

(or *How to Think like a Homeless Father)*

Think of every material thing, as a tiny hook.
A way to keep your grip on life.

Think of the gifts you buy at Christmas time
to be unwrapped in the morning.

Think of your family sitting around, like in an old painting
of nomads sitting beside animal skins or scalps.

Think of that celebration, the counting of those spoils.
Your reward at the end of a long year.
The things you did to make it through the winter.

Think of the dollhouse you bought for your daughter
so huge, it loomed over all of the other presents.

Think of the neighbours knocking
at your front door to gasp in awe.
Think of her little cousin's pupils dilated with envy.

Picture the pleasure of putting that dollhouse together,
one of the last things you do before it all falls apart.

Now think of your daughter crying about the dollhouse
while you walk the streets, or sleep in your car.
Everything you own packed into a storage space
like tokens in a shrine.

Think of the furniture you sat together on,
your favourite knife and fork,
framed photographs of holidays and birthday parties.

And think of the Dollhouse sitting there,
holding its own under all that weight.

Think of that pressure everyday.

3

River Son

I dreamt of my boy sinking into the river
to drown or so we thought. I panicked,
dived in, thinking he'd already be dead
and found him walking along the riverbed.

In the glimmering realm of rivertime,
green-slick stones and golden light,
his mouth opened in a silent scream
that sang of the void in him and me.

No air went in, no bubbles escaped.
I wrapped him in my arms and pressed
his lips to mine to fill them with life,
all that I know in this world to be right.

Rain

There's nothing I like better
than this city in the rain.
If you go with the flow
let the weather have its way.

The trees all screaming gratitude,
their leaves like opened palms.
Trapped cars humming in their lanes,
radios and wipers on.

The Liffey drinking everything
from the sky into its stream.
Tributes as little rivulets
in pilgrimage to the sea.

Hemlock and rapeseed nodding us on,
the grass a chaos of blades,
as we carry the weight of the clouds
like a steel helmet on our day.

Nature opening like a drinking mouth,
the roads all slick and grey.
There's nothing I like better
than this city in the rain.

Shebeen Shaman

You've got the city stitched up
as a kip drowned in cynicism, then
your head's blown open by a skinful
of pills and sweet Jesus, tonight man
the DJ's got the skills. There's poets
on the dancefloor, off their face on yokes
braying, yo DJ turn it up, let's drown
out this island's sense of failure.

In the smoker young bankers suck
cocaine from a stool. Gangs sit
around eating Chinese, a man fingers
his friend's wife on the sofa.
Left after the dance hall, following
the small crowd, you'll find her there
despite yourself, an aging girl
in this illegal rave, calling out to passing strangers.

"Hey you, you are going to be a Da in two weeks."
"Hey you, I know you're a twin, but you shoulda been a triplet."

Secrets nobody has told her.
She's never wrong.
You see, she overdosed on L.S.D.
Heard voices from the crypt in her teens.
One night after the Beat on the Street
she stuck her ear to the cross
shaped window of a church basement
and our misery poured out in dead whispers.
Walking home, all the shadows
in the trees were demonic dogs, holy
Mary statues barked after her on the street.
Her soul exploded like popcorn
as she was blown through the city at witching hour.

Now she's all grown up, a new cliché
for the modern age of D.N.A. and troikas.
Modern Dublin's Molly Malone
with an electric aura and her cleavage showing.

Approach her at your peril.
She's seen the underside of Sides.
Went out on the tide of too many parties.
Took nine E back when 'e's were capital 'E's.
Knows the hard centre of the human stain.
Knows what you won't even admit to yourself.
Best to keep away from her
and the shebeens that sell
cocaine, MDMA and hope.
She sees you coming.
She's all you won't tell of Dublin's secrets.
There but not there, always.
Like the spaces in the rain.

Pawned

Now is the hour of who gives a fuck.
The good all dead, the living all rusted
synapses, half metalled eyes,
melting into mobile phones,
thumbs glued to handheld familiars.

I bang the keys built from light and pixels.
Everything I touch a reflection of nothing.
Making monkey-speak as I stumble
towards a city I made of dreams.

All roads lead to posterity street.
Which still exists if you listen to billboards.
A troll clasps each of my skinny-jeaned legs.
One a pregnant wolf called debt.
The other a bog koala – chomping at my knee.
All this is the price of poetry.

No money in it, but much to weigh –
the sun, the hearts of people,
the going rate for wedding rings.
I just dropped mine off in the pawn shop.
I didn't get as much as I thought.
Nobody ever does.

Little Tug

Between our destination –

Lambay Island,

and the beach.

(and feeling the pull of each)

Me and my friends,

in kayaks skimming

across the sea –

saw a bee.

Dancing

there is no time only now
there is no age only here
between all these people
we work around each other

a subtle gravity pulls at us
pushing us apart
drawing us together
under the strobes

beat vibrates across the floor
into our feet
into our hips
into our hearts hanging
loose in our ribcages

breath shaken from our lips
ecstasy lifts
the heat of sweat
a glimpse of skin
in everyone's mind
sweet friction

every breath a maybe
every clap a yes
each step we're taking
bringing us together

Heat

My finger running from the knee to the feet

along the shin, the prickle of skin.

The blood racing along our hearts

within this moment.

The breath between your parted lips.

Your clavicle under my fingertips.

A series of openings,

things unhitched, unclasped,

others grasped, constricted.

I admit I'm yours,

you say you're mine.

It's all so clichéd, so sublime,

so ordinary, divine.

Fronds

As the fronds of an uprooted fern
will crave the air they left;
the memory of wetter
weather say, the heather
clinging to spongy earth,
the sense of tannin coloured
water running over rocks
licked smooth by glaciers.

So the fabric of unbuttoned clothes
smolder in your wardrobe
for the swirl of elsewhere;
a hand felt on a dancefloor,
skin brushed in a corridor,
a cheek against your neck.

And the air here still
holds your breath,
will not forget being
moved by your words;
the mark of you
in a silent room.

Liminal

Sunday – it's hard to get up.
Put my feet to the floor and rise.
Walking into who knows what.
To arrive again between two states.
The feeling of everything falling away
wanting something to come along.

Sit and open up the old laptop.
Fuck around with some metaphors.
Stitch meaning to where there is none.
Bind things together that shouldn't go.
Death to rainbows, loss to hope.

My children watch from the sofa.
Looking up at me like I'm a god.
My heart is a bucket
lowered into a well.
How far down before there is water?

4

Distraction

Today it's in a bottle,
tomorrow it's on television –
some new series you have
to keep watching, day after
that it's in a cigarette, or
between another woman's legs.

You think it's the taste of
youth, or risk, but it's
just one trek towards
the point you seek,
furthest away from yourself –
all that you could have been.

Beyond This.

Beyond Spanish granite, beyond hanging lights,

beyond thirteen concrete V-beams, beyond panoramic views,

beyond this interplay of people, stone, and silence,

I'm thinking of one thing, when I think of this place.

Above us in space, the Perseids,

trailing in the wake of the Swift-Tuttle comet,

ejected particles, celestial debris,

arrive here yearly, in our Summer season.

I'm thinking, do those meteors impact on us

or does our Earth move towards them, and scoop them up?

And in the way we can't really call south the bottom

or in the way we can't really call north the top,

beyond our mapping of this cosmic choreography,

we don't know what draws what to what.

I'm thinking, that's the way we go through books.

That's the way books move through us.

And if readers are made up of all that they borrow

and a book is the sum of all of its writer's read words

then what this library stores beyond its many-thousand covers

is as great as all we make and hold inside of us.

The gift of this place transcends time, and distance.

Its gift is our potential, and potentially infinite.

Nothing Better

Nothing better explained about us
than the way the sun shone down
three hundred million years ago
on trees that drank the light
and died
and died
in the mouths of dinosaurs,
in the thundering roar
of a fallen comet that tore up the world.

Nothing better explained about us
than how millennia after that
we tapped into those trees black remains
and built a world from it.
How we put that juice of the past in a car
(just some metal box
of glass and speed and magic)
and set it on fire.

Nothing better explained about us
than how we ride that tiny explosion
into town for something we forgot.
Something that lived before as well.
Something we plucked or murdered.
Something that we don't really like
but has to be hunted down because
it goes well with the right wine.

Dáil Question

In the centre
of the chamber
a gigantic shit.
And nobody is
owning up to it.

Caledonia

The fire was low, almost burnt out
just like us after hours of laughter,
drinks, and craic.

The sky had brightened and we looked up
at what we thought were planes.
Three vapour trails in the sky above
but then we saw the orange glow
three criss crossing meteors burning out.

All our phones were dead,
I was too drunk to remember the chords of any songs
There are no photos.
Just this.

We'd hollowed out the night like
our ancestors glean the marrow from the bone.

Morning Curse

Amber amphitheatre of the dawn.

Underbelly of clouds.

Burnt orange tundra

of upside down drumlins.

This is all I'm cursed with in the morning,

beauty infecting me with the question;

what does evolution have to gain

from a man who'd run away

from everything to be closer to the stars?

Randomer

January

This just in.
I'm on a Dublin bus into town,
forty years in this skin,
still in awe of traffic, streetlights,
the girl that sits to my right
twenty years younger than me –
same age as those soldiers
honoured in the park outside.

Branches are scraping the window,
like people who'll never learn, no matter
how often they're slapped in the face.

I'm coming up to Heuston station.
Named after some dude from before now,
before everything became such a glorious mess
of colour and life and death and people.

I'm about to cross over the Liffey.
On my way to a meeting
where I learn to sell myself
without sounding too desperate.

The inspectors have been on
punching our tickets.
Mine only gets me to the river.
After that my credit runs out
And I'm going to have to wing it.

This just in.
It's snowing outside. Flakes aborting
their mission to stay gorgeous.
Seeping into the ground and
slowly steaming into the sky.

I just crossed a bridge – underneath lies
the road to Chapelizod.
Last time I was parked there
the Spar was held up by a two hooded men.
One had a hammer, one had a sword.
It's not something I could do.
But I've considered it.

My infractions are smaller.
A slammed door.
A smashed glass.
A shout getting swallowed,
to mix with toxins that might cause cancer.

This just in.
My body says –
this guy's a snowflake.
My antibodies are cartoons complaining
of not being born in a better place, a better day
when my blood rushed faster.
When afterwards was just another word
for what's next and nothing to do
with the darkness outside.
The broken light in my garden.
The man waiting round the corner
in a stolen car, his hand on a Glock.
A face like mine folded into his wallet.

February

This just in.
I found out about a boy allergic to lemons
If life gives him lemons, he dies.

I'm on my way to an illegal reading.
A poetry sit-in in a squat.
Last night I watched a video of refugees
running from the French riot squad.
Tear gas rocketed through the air –
meteors seen at dawn.
They grabbed whatever they could,
the Jungle burning down around them.
Not clothes, not the paraphernalia of exile,
but weapons – sticks, poles, bits of fencing.
They ran into the motorway
onto a truck mired in the chaos
and started to attack this ark.
Every door bolted closed
while they throw concrete
through the windscreen.

Just just in.
I'm seventeen again watching the L.A. riots.
Hearing the easy cries –
how could they, savages, animals.
I'm watching this all and my friend is there.
Open arms just trying to help
or understand at least,
acknowledge all these wrongs.
A Pregnant woman beaten with a baton.
All the lost children.

The poetry in the squat
is like the second act of a still unfinished play.
Earlier the stage was set for hope
until the Gardai bulldozed it all
at four in the morning.

The poet on stage is a Dublin girl.
Bright, young, gorgeous.
What does she and the refugee have in common?
Hard to know until they sit down and talk.
All I know is that they're both in the front row
of a show that's forever collapsing.

All of this is connected I'm sure but
I'm not smart enough to know why.
I'm just some randomer among randomers
throwing out words and seeing what flies.

December

This just in.
Bus Éireann bus back to Dublin
The roads of Ireland are grey and slick with rain
and the weather forecast is nothing but
the same numb pain for the next few years.

We're running for the hills but there are no hills.
Nothing but the bleak American tundra of capitalism.
A cartoon in the white house for us all to laugh and cry at.

At least it's spring now and the trees are singing again.
Gnarling their bark as they stretch towards the sky.
Leaves throwing out oxygen.
Our small white ring around our blue pearl
of Earth hanging in the blackness.

This just in.
The bus just overtook a chemical truck.
The driver, beer-fat, maybe
from danger money that he spends
on drink to cope with the fact that he drives
explosives all over the country – or
that one drunk driver
or one blown out tyre could send him
flying through the sky with fire for wings.

There's a line of birch outside –
our tall standing brothers.
I can feel them watching, swaying,
saying our time is up or almost up.

Tired I close my eyes.
My mind calls up the sea.
The sound of its stillness.
The wind dies down.
The slick ripple as a cormorant
dives under the surface.

Here we are now in the underworld
of what's not understood with words
but known by the body.
The erotic touch of the water on skin.
Goose pimples rising.
Language leaves me.
I lie back and sleep.
Next stop the cobbled streets of Dublin.

Sea of Green

Like a chorus around a small buttercup.

On the arms of a thistle as it reaches up.

The shock of it catching in my open throat.

Gleaming in the wind of a sycamore tree.

Running the rail line, a burst of sharp leaves.

Tearing at an old pile of rotting sleepers.

Licking at the blue of a glimmering stream.

Firework bursts at the end of each tree.

Dark and unfurled, yellow underneath.

Crushed under tractor, hoof, foot, bent knee.

A cast of thousands under scattered rapeseed.

Mattress under rump of a sleeping cow.

Blanket of one colour, on and out.

Clump, bush, shrub, tuft.

All of it bursting out and up at once.

Stalk, blade, bloom, glade.

All of it singing along to the same song.

Rolling over hill, over valley, every way.

All across the country all across the world.

Stalk, blade, bloom, frond.

On, and on, and on, and on.

COLM KEEGAN is a writer and poet from Dublin, Ireland. Since 2005, he has been shortlisted four times for the Hennessy New Irish Writing Award, for both poetry and fiction and won the All Ireland Poetry Slam in 2010. His first book *Don't Go There* (also with Salmon) was released to critical acclaim in 2012.

In 2014 he was awarded a residency in the LexIcon, Ireland's largest public library. He has developed numerous creative writing projects for schools and colleges across the country. He is a creative writing teacher and co-founder of the Inklinks Project, a creative writing initiative for young writers.

In 2011, he was nominated for the Dublin Fringe's 'Little Gem' Award for the spoken-word play *Three Men Talking About Things They Kinda Know About* – which has toured Ireland and sold out in Bristol, London and Paris. His play For Saoirse was staged in the Axis Theatre in 2016. In January 2017 his short play, The Process was staged in the Abbey Theatre as part of 24 Hour Plays. He also writes for television.

He was a co-founder and board member of Lingo, Ireland's first Spoken Word festival.

Photograph: Jessica Ryan

"Like the sea-run Steelhead salmon that thrashes upstream to its spawning ground, then instead of dying, returns to the sea – Salmon Poetry Press brings precious cargo to both Ireland and America in the poetry it publishes, then carries that select work to its readership against incalculable odds."

TESS GALLAGHER